F O U N

PRAYER MINISTR

Prophetic Prayer
Mini-Course
"Living a Prophetic Lifestyle"

by Denny Finnegan

PUBLISHED BY EXCELLENT PRESS
FROM EXCELLENT ADVENTURES!, INC
ATLANTA, GEORGIA, U.S.A
PRINTED IN THE U.S.A.

Excellent Press is a subsidiary of Excellent Adventures!, Inc.
Excellent Adventures!,Inc. is dedicated to serving the local
church and missional organizations. We believe God's vision
for this division of Excellent Adventures!, Inc. is to provide
church leaders and pastors with biblical, user-friendly
materials that will help them evangelize, disciple and minister
to children, youth and families. We are also dedicated to
serving first time authors of Christian books and materials.

It is our prayer that this workbook from Excellent Press will
help you discover Biblical truths for your own life ad help you
meet the needs of others. May God richly bless you.

For more information about Excellent Press, please contact
Joe Schlosser at 1 - 888 - 740 - 4834 or by email at
joseph@schlosser.com

All scripture quotations, unless otherwise indicated, are taken
from the HOLY BIBLE, NEW INTERNATIONAL
VERSION (NIV) Copyright © 1973, 1978, 1984 by
International Bible Society.
Used by permission of Zondervan. All rights reserved.

Scripture quotations marked NAU are taken from the New
American Updated Version of the Holy Bible.

ISBN: 978-0-9889584-5-6

Cover design and interior layout by Joe Schlosser.
www.DennyFinnegan.com
www.GoAheadLaunch.com

DEDICATION

I was involved with Prophetic Prayer long before I knew what it was. I only knew that I sensed God's leading in how I should pray, and then sought to be obedient. It took the encouragement of various authors like Graham Cooke, Kris Vallotton, Cindy Jacobs and Bill Hamon, to be able to understand and articulate how God was using me and working through me to minister to others.

Yet I cannot forget to express how grateful I am to the numerous friends God brought into my life over the years that affirmed and exhorted me to develop the prophetic gifts they discerned the Holy Spirit had placed within me. There are too many to mention just within this dedication!

I praise God for how the Body of Christ builds up, exhorts and comforts when it allows the prophetic to operate as God designed it to do so. I have been blessed because of those who were obedient to the Lord.

Pastor Denny Finnegan

Table of Contents

FORWARD

I would not call myself a prophet. But I know that I minister prophetically. And I believe it is the Lord's desire for all His children to walk in the prophetic (cf., 1 Corinthians 14:1,5). Because at the heart of the prophetic is God's desire for us to *hear* His voice and to be *guided* by His voice; at the heart of the prophetic is God's desire for us to minister His love to others; at the heart of the prophetic we will find the Heart of God.

Here are just a three reasons why I believe that the prophetic is *still for today*:

First, the Bible *is* God's Word to us. But, in harmony with the truth of the Bible, it is not the only way God continues to actively speak to His people today. A basic principle of the prophetic movement, and a truth supported by the Bible, is that "*God actively speaks into the lives of His people.*" And that makes sense! Because our God is a "God of relationship". Practically and logically speaking, why would God create human beings for relationship with Him, and then cease to actively speak into the lives of the ones He loves?

Second, if we don't believe in the prophetic and that God still speaks *to us* or *through us* today, then why do we still pray for guidance for ourselves and for others? Prayers, for "guidance and illumination," presupposes that *God will answer our prayer*. While God does give guidance through the scriptures, the scriptures clearly declare that God also chooses to use other means to reveal His will and heart to us that are consistent with His truths found in the scriptures.

Third, this seven-week course, divided into three sections, comes as a result of a reflection of how God has been growing me in a "prophetic lifestyle". He has continuously been at work both to help me grow in my intimacy with Him and grow in my service to Him.

And the "prophetic" has been an important part of both of these areas of growth.

The purpose of this study is to help you grow in confidence: 1) that God still speaks today *to you*; and, 2) that God still speaks today *through you*. All of us can be "prophetic"!

The Apostle Paul wrote in 1 Corinthians 14:1, "*Pursue love, yet earnestly desire spiritual gifts, **but especially that you may prophesy***" (NAU) Paul had an expectation for everyone to operate in the "prophetic".

The Apostle Paul also wrote two verses later, in 1 Corinthians 14:3, "*But everyone who prophesies speaks to men for their strengthening, encouragement and comfort.*" Think of how powerfully the prophetic can help us speak with relevancy to our times, to our culture and to our generation, while also helping us to meaningfully fulfill Jesus' great commission in Luke 4:18-19, and revealed more fully in Isaiah 61:1-3:

> "1 *The Spirit of the Lord GOD is upon me, Because the LORD has anointed me To bring good news to the afflicted; He has sent me to bind up the brokenhearted, To proclaim liberty to captives And freedom to prisoners; 2 To proclaim the favorable year of the LORD And the day of vengeance of our God; To comfort all who mourn, 3 To grant those who mourn in Zion, Giving them a garland instead of ashes, The oil of gladness instead of mourning, The mantle of praise instead of a spirit of fainting. So they will be called oaks of righteousness, The planting of the LORD, that He may be glorified.*" (Isaiah 61:1-3)

You can be prophetic! And, you can live a prophetic lifestyle!

~ *Pastor Denny Finnegan*

SUGGESTED STUDY TRACK OPTIONS

Class Schedule:

Lesson 1:   Foundations for A Prophetic Lifestyle - Part 1: *"On-Growing Intimacy with God"*

Lesson 2:   Foundations for A Prophetic Lifestyle - Part 2: "Learning to *'Wait Upon the Lord'"*

Lesson 3:   Ways God Reveals His Heart to Us - Part 1: *"An Introduction"*

Lesson 4:   Ways God Reveals His Heart to Us - Part 2: *"God Gives Spiritual Gifts"*

Lesson 5:   Ways God Reveals His Heart to Us - Part 3: *"God Uses 'The Testimony of Jesus'"*

Lesson 6:   Ways God Reveals His Heart to Us - Part 4: *"God Uses Dreams and Visions"*

Lesson 7:   Living a Prophetic Lifestyle: *"Ministering to Others Prophetically"*

Appendix: "Listening Prayer Exercises"

Study Tracks Overview:

1. Study Track Option #1: Suggested format for a Sunday School Class Setting

   Laying a Biblical Foundation - 30 minutes
   Practicing What We Have Been Taught - 20 minutes
   "Praying for Vision" - 10 minutes

2. Study Track Option #2: Suggested format for a Small Group Setting

   "Check-In" Time – 10 minutes
   Laying a Biblical Foundation - 45 minutes
   Practicing What We Have Been Taught - 25 minutes
   "Praying for Vision" - 10 minutes

3. Study Track Option #3: Suggested for an "extended Sunday School Class Setting". The purpose is to allow for greater experience in "listening prayer"

   Break each lesson into "two parts" over 2 Sundays:

   Part 1 – "Check-in" – 10 minutes
     Laying a Biblical Foundation – 40 minutes
     Close in Prayer for Each Other – 10 minutes

   Part 2 – "Check-in" – 10 minutes
     Practicing What We Have Been Taught – 40 minutes
     "Praying for Vision" – 10 Minutes

SECTION 1 : "Foundations for a Prophetic Lifestyle"

Lesson 1: Foundations for A Prophetic Lifestyle
Part 1: "On-Growing Intimacy with God"

Lesson 2: Foundations for A Prophetic Lifestyle
Part 2: "Learning to Wait Upon the Lord"

LESSON 1 :   Foundations for a Prophetic Lifestyle – Part 1: "On-Growing Intimacy With God

Laying a Biblical Foundation

How Jesus *"Kept the Main Thing the Main Thing!*

Through the years, I've heard many whom I admire in the Kingdom of God make a common statement about ministry; that is, how important it is *"to keep the main thing the main thing!"*

When I think about how Jesus exemplified this - *"keeping the main thing the main thing"* - out of the many examples of what Jesus said, taught and did, there are two specific passages from the New Testament that continue to have a powerful impact upon my life:

> "35 *Jesus was going through all the cities and villages, teaching in their synagogues and proclaiming the gospel of the kingdom, and healing every kind of disease and every kind of sickness. 36 Seeing the people, He felt compassion for them, because they were distressed and dispirited like sheep without a shepherd."*   (Matthew 9:35-36, NAS)

> "19 *Therefore Jesus answered and was saying to them, 'Truly, truly, I say to you, the Son can do nothing of Himself, unless it is something He sees the Father doing; for whatever the Father does, these things the Son also does in like manner. 20 For the Father loves the Son, and shows Him all*

*things that He Himself is doing; and the Father
will show Him greater works than these, so that
you will marvel. ""*

(John 5:19-20, NAS)

Matthew 9:35-36:

1. The Greek word for *"He felt compassion ... "* could
literally translate as *"His guts ached ... "*.

    - What was it about these people that stirred
    Jesus' *compassion*?

    _____

    _____

    _____

    - How does Jesus' *compassion* connect to Jesus
    mission and commission?

    _____

    _____

    _____

    - How does Jesus' *compassion* in us connect to
    our mission and commission?

    _____

    _____

    _____

2. According to Matthew 9:35-36, *"What is the main
thing"* to Jesus? How did Jesus *"keep the main thing the
main thing"*?

    _____

    _____

    _____

    _____

    _____

John 5:19-20:

3. In this passage, Jesus describes "the source of His Mission and Commission".

> \- How does Jesus describe His relationship with God, the Father and Jesus, the Son?

> _____
> _____
> _____

> \- What does that imply about our relationship with God, the Father and Jesus, the Son?

> _____
> _____
> _____

How We Can *"Keep the Main Thing the Main Thing!*

Two more passages us for us to compare ...

> *"Love the LORD your God with all your heart and with all your soul and with all your strength."*
>
> (Deuteronomy 6:5, NIV)

> *"We love, because He first loved us."* (1 John 4:19, NIV)

God does *not* ask anything *from us* that He has not already done *for us*!

1. How should this truth encourage us to pursue *God's love for us* and pursue *giving our love back to God*?

_____

_____

_____

_____

_____

_____

2. How do these verses help us to stay focused in following Jesus?

_____

_____

_____

_____

_____

_____

3. How do you let God love you? How do you respond in love to God?

_____

_____

_____

_____

_____

_____

Practicing What We Have Been Taught

Praying and praising through Scripture has been one very "practical" and "helpful" means for me to draw closer to the heart of God, something I have been more intentional practicing and pursuing over the past 10+ years. For the next 20 minutes, each one of us is going to practice *letting God love us* and practice *giving our love back to God.*

Psalm 139:1-6:

1. Open up to Psalm 139:1-6. Find a place where you will not be distracted by others.

2. Ask the Holy Spirit to help you. Speak each verse to God as if they are *your own words* to God. After you speak each verse, stop and spend time thanking God as the Holy Spirit shows how it is *personally true for you!*

3. Journal what the Lord shows you.

4. Spend as much time as you need with each verse, even if you don't get past verse 1.

Praying for Vision

1. Find a prayer partner for this part of the lesson.

2. Pray for each other asking the Holy Spirit to show you the places, people and/or "divine appointments" the Spirit has/is setting up for you. Also ask how the Lord would have you offer His encouragement to them.

3. In your prayers for each other, make sure you include

asking the Holy Spirit for the empowerment and resources to do what you are being led to do.

4. "Debrief" with each other after you are finished praying and discuss how you can hold one another accountable for what you believe the Spirit is asking you to do ... make sure you exchange phone numbers so you can talk during the week.

5. If you do *not* get a clear sense of anything, *that's okay ... it happens to me, too*! Persist in prayer for clarity during the week for yourself and for your prayer partner.

LESSON 2 : Foundations for a Prophetic Lifestyle – Part 2: Learning to "Wait Upon The Lord"

In talking about *the prophetic*, we are talking about the ways God speaks to us. In laying a *Foundation for A Prophetic Lifestyle*, we are talking about the ways we position ourselves *to hear God when He speaks* to us. The previous lesson is meant to help us position ourselves "in a relationship of love" with God; this lesson is meant to help us position ourselves "in a relationship of listening" with God.

"Listening to God" is not something that comes easy for me, because I tend to be more of a "human doing" than a "human being" with God! Over the past 10 plus years, the Lord has been working on me to learn how to just "be with Him" - the words "wait upon the Lord" describe very well this concept. I believe that our "relationship of love" with God and our "relationship of listening" with God are meant to be two very important keys for our service to God.

If we change the way we view prayer to be first and foremost as communion with God, then heaven and earth meet through us. First we minister *to* God, then we are better able to minister *for* God.

Let's look at some of what I have been discovering about what it means to *"Wait Upon the Lord."*

What It Means to *Wait Upon the Lord*:

1. "5 *I **wait** for the LORD, my soul does **wait**, And in His word do I hope. 6 My soul **waits** for the Lord More than the watchmen for the morning; Indeed, more than the watchmen for the morning.*" (Psalm 130:5-6, NIV) The Hebrew word used for *"wait"*, could also translate as, *"hope or look for"*.

    - What do you learn about ***what*** it means to "*wait upon the Lord*" in these verses?

_____

_____

_____

_____

_____

_____

2. "*In the morning, O LORD, you hear my voice; in the morning I lay my requests before you and **wait** in expectation.*" (Psalm 5:3, NIV) The Hebrew word used for *"wait"* could also translate as, *"eagerly watch, post a lookout."*

    - What do you learn about ***what*** it means to "*wait upon the Lord*" in this verses?

_____

_____

_____

_____

_____

_____

Why We Should _Wait Upon the Lord_:

1. _"Yet the LORD longs to be gracious to you; he rises to show you compassion. For the LORD is a God of justice. Blessed are all who **wait** for him!"_ (Isaiah 30:18, NIV) The Hebrew word used for _"wait"_ can also mean, _"tarry; wait in ambush."_

> - What do you learn about **_why_** we should _"wait upon the Lord"_ in this verse?

> _____
> _____
> _____
> _____
> _____
> _____

2. Yet those who wait for the LORD will gain new strength; They will mount up with wings like eagles, They will run and not get tired, They will walk and not become weary. (Isaiah 40:31, NAU version) Same Hebrew word used as in Psalm 130:5-6.

> - What do you learn about **_why_** we should _"wait upon the Lord"_ in this verse?

> _____
> _____
> _____
> _____
> _____
> _____

How We Should *Wait Upon the Lord*:

These two verses do not contain the word *"wait"*, but carry the concept, and have been two of many important verses God has been using to teach me **how** *to wait upon Him.*

1. *"**Be still**, and know that I am God; I will be exalted among the nations, I will be exalted in the earth.*" (Psalm 46:10) The Hebrew word used for *"be still"* could also translate as, *"sink down, relax, cease striving, withdraw".*

- What do you learn about **how** we should *"wait upon the Lord*" in this verse.

_____
_____
_____
_____
_____
_____

2. *"O God, you are my God, **earnestly I seek you; my soul thirsts for you, my body longs for you**, in a dry and weary land where there is no water.*" [(Psalm 63:1) A psalm of David. When he was in the Desert of Judah.] Compare David's imagery with his location.

- What do you learn about **how** we should *"wait upon the Lord*" in this verse?

_____
_____
_____
_____
_____
_____

Practicing What We Have Been Taught

We are going to take what we have learnt above, and now spend some time personally applying it. But so as to create an environment of "uninterrupted flow", we will be combining all three aspects together - *what, why* and *how*.

There are two particular verses that have been both helpful and meaningful to me, and three particular statements of desire I use to surrender myself to Jesus. Use what is useful to you. Then simply *"wait"* - let Jesus respond to you, and then respond back to Him.

Take the risk to *"wait upon the Lord"*, and journal anything you wish!

Verses to Reflect Upon:

"Delight yourself in the LORD ...."
(Psalm 37:4a);

" ...fixing our eyes on Jesus, the author and perfecter of faith, who for the joy set before Him..."
(Hebrews 12:2)

Statements of Desire to Reflect Upon:

"What's on your heart, Lord Jesus?"

"What will give you delight or joy in this time?"

"What do you desire out of this time with me?"

Praying for Vision

1. Find a prayer partner for this part of the lesson.

2. Pray for each other asking the Holy Spirit to show you the places, people and/or "divine appointments" the Spirit has/is setting up for you. Also ask how the Lord would have you offer His encouragement to them.

3. In your prayers for each other, make sure you include asking the Holy Spirit for the empowerment and resources to do what you are being led to do.

4. "Debrief" with each other after you are finished praying and discuss how you can hold one another accountable for what you believe the Spirit is asking you to do ... make sure you exchange phone numbers so you can talk during the week.

5. If you do *not* get a clear sense of anything, *that's okay ... it happens to me, too*! Persist in prayer for clarity during the week for yourself and for your prayer partner.

SECTION 2 : "Ways God Reveals His Heart to Us"

LESSON 3: Ways God Reveals His Heart to Us
- **Part 1:** "An Introduction"

LESSON 4: Ways God Reveals His Heart to Us
- **Part 2:** "God Gives Spiritual Gifts"

LESSON 5: Ways God Reveals His Heart to Us
- **Part 3:** "God Uses 'The Testimony of Jesus'"

LESSON 6: Ways God Reveals His Heart to Us
- **Part 4:** "God Uses Dreams and Visions"

LESSON 3 : Ways God Reveals His Heart to Us - Part 1: "An Introduction"

"Pursue love, yet desire earnestly spiritual gifts, but especially that you may prophesy."
(1 Corinthians 14:1, NAU)

As we begin this middle section on *Ways God Reveals His Heart to Us*, there are **five things** that I believe are important for us to keep in mind:

Point#1:

> "4 ***Now there are varieties of gifts, but the same Spirit.*** *5 And there are varieties of ministries, and the same Lord. 6 There are varieties of effects, but the same God who works all things in all persons. 7 But to each one is given the manifestation of the Spirit for the common good. 8 For to one is given the word of wisdom through the Spirit, and to another the word of knowledge according to the same Spirit; 9 to another faith by the same Spirit, and to another gifts of healing by the one Spirit, 10 and to another the effecting of miracles, and to another prophecy, and to another the distinguishing of spirits, to another various kinds of tongues, and to another the interpretation of tongues. 11* ***But one and the same Spirit works all these things, distributing to each one individually just as He wills.***"
(1 Corinthians 12:4-11,NAU)

There is not full agreement between various

ministries, prophetic or otherwise, on what should be included as prophetic gifts, as well as, how these gifts manifest. The particular spiritual gifts I have selected to present to you come from the Apostle Paul's list in 1 Corinthians 12:4-11: *word of wisdom, word of knowledge, prophecy, discernment of spirits,* and *interpretation of tongues.* This list is the result of a combination of my studies, training with some prophetic ministries, and from my own personal experiences with the Holy Spirit going back to when I became a follower of Jesus in 1971.

Point #2: It is important that we *desire earnestly* to be used by God. In 1 Corinthians 14:1, the Apostle Paul strongly encourages us to *"**desire earnestly** spiritual gifts,..."* The Greek word used for *"desire earnestly"* can also translate as, "be jealous of; set one's heart on, be deeply concerned about; have or show great interest in; perhaps covet (e.g., James 4:2)."

Through the years of my walk of faith, it has been my experience that if I am eager to serve the Lord, the Lord has wonderfully provided me with both the resources and the opportunity to do so. When I have been complacent about God and His Kingdom, the Lord has *still* been very interested in providing me both the opportunity and the resources to serve Him... but it is *still* my responsibility to *"seek first His kingdom"*!

Point #3: It is important that we *desire to hear* what is on God's Heart. In 1 Corinthians 14:1, the Apostle Paul also strongly encourages us in our *"earnest desire"* for *"spiritual gifts"* *"... **especially** that you may prophesy."* Why would Paul encourage us to do *anything* for the Lord that Paul did not personally believe and know was possible for us to receive and achieve? That is true for any command of God through Jesus Christ and in the power of the Holy Spirit.

We can hear God! But *do we want to?* In Jeremiah 29:13, God has made a promise to us that, *"You will seek Me and find Me when you seek me with all your heart."* God wants to be found by us. But when we find God, according to His promise, why would God then remain *mute*? That would be contradictory to both God's promise and God's nature. God especially desires to speak to those who desire to hear what He has to say!

Point #4: It is important that we *strengthen our faith to believe* God wants to speak to you and through you. I used to play all sorts of "mind games" with myself: *"What if I mess up in hearing God? What if I don't have the faith or the ability to hear God? What if God thinks I'm a pest or annoying Him all the time?* etc..."

During one of my "worry sessions" that was supposed to have been a time a prayer, I sensed God saying to me, *"Why are you more impressed with yourself than with Me?!?"* **Ouch!**

But lest you worry that you don't have what it takes to hear God, here is a reminder of three principles of prayer God continues to teach me to believe ... *and rejoice in.* They are listed in the introduction to the *Foundations for Prayer Ministry in the Local Church* material:

> 1) ***God's ability to communicate*** *with us will always be greater than our inability to hear -* God is *not limited* by our ability when God wants to communicate with us.

2) ***God's desire to communicate*** *with us will always be stronger than whatever we may believe about God at any given moment* - God is *not deterred* by our lack of desire when God wants to relate to us.

3) ***God's delight to communicate*** *with us will always be 'immeasurably more than all we ask or imagine, according to His power that is at work within us'* (Ephesians 3:20) - God is *not disappointed* in us, because *God chose us* to be His children.

The desire for the prophetic begins with our desire to hear God and His words of love *to us* and *through us* to others.

Point#5: *Finally*, it is important that we are *willing to take risks*. I remember one instance where the Holy Spirit was teaching me "to trust" and "to risk" with the spiritual gifts I sensed I had been given. It was in a small group setting where we were all seeking to learn more about the gifts of the Holy Spirit. Much of this was still very new to me and I still very much wanted to learn, yet *I was in charge of leading the group!*

I sensed the Holy Spirit giving me a word of discernment for one of the people in the group... don't ask me which spiritual gift it was, because I can't remember what I spoke to them. I just know it was not the "gift of tongues" with its "interpretation". As soon as I took the risk of speaking it to them, there came into my mind and heart a word of discernment for everyone else in the group.

In asking them afterwards if they sensed the Lord

speaking to them through these "words", each one confirmed that it had ministered to them. In spite of my lack of my lack of experience and shaky confidence in such new ways of ministry, God graciously ministered to them as well as to me. In this situation and in many others, I have learned the importance of taking a risk for the Lord so that I might not miss out on an opportunity to bring His *"strengthening, encouragement and comfort"* to someone else (cf. 1 Corinthians 14:3).

It is okay to make mistakes if we approach the exercise of our gifts with a true humility before God and with a true confidence in *"the surpassing greatness of the power is of God and not of ourselves"* (cf. 2 Cor.4:7). God will always be greater than our abilities and our mistakes!

Discussion Questions:

Take as much time as you need to in each section. You do *not* have to finish all of them during this class... you can finish them later! Give God a chance to speak *to you* and *through you*. The five sections of questions correspond to the five points above.

1) What do you believe about the spiritual gifts selected for our study? How have you seen the Holy Spirit manifest them in your own life? How would you like to see the Holy Spirit manifest them in your life?

2) How do you desire to serve God and His Kingdom? Of the spiritual gifts we will be looking at, what spiritual gifts do you *earnestly desire* of the Holy Spirit? Which of theses scare you or intimidate you?

3) What are some of the things you do to position

yourself to hear God? On a scale of 1- 10, how would you rate your *eagerness* to hear God, and why?

4) What do you believe about God's desire to speak to you? What are some of your joys in this?   What are some of your challenges?

5) When it comes to taking risks for God, on a scale of 1- 10, how would you rate yourself? What is one of your fears in serving God? What is one of your hopes in serving God?

Close in Prayer for each other. For those desiring to receive a particular spiritual gift that we have listed, *pray for them in faith* that the Holy Spirit wants to impart to them. But practice listening to the Holy Spirit as you pray.

LESSON 4: <u>Ways God Reveals His Heart to Us - Part 2:</u> " God Gives Spiritual Gifts

This lesson will look at five spiritual gifts God uses to reveal His Heart to us as He ministers *to us* or *through us* that are considered revelatory in nature mentioned in I Corinthians 12:4-11: *word of wisdom, word of knowledge, prophecy, discernment of spirits,* and *interpretation of tongues.* I personally have seen and experienced how these particular spiritual gifts are "revelatory" in nature, and how God has used them *through me* and *through others* to speak God's heart *"for strengthening, encouragement and comfort"* (cf. 1 Cor.14:3).

The words "prophesy" and "prophecy" (*naba* - main Hebrew root word; *propheteuo* - main Greek root word) both carry with it the idea that you are "under the influence of a divine spirit" and where you might "speak a message" for this divine spirit; it even included teaching under divine inspiration. These words were used to describe "the giving of divine revelation". In a strict sense, prophecy is defined to include *foretelling* - "speaking to the future", and *forth-telling* - "speaking to the present". (Two examples of *foretelling* are Isaiah 16:5 and Acts 11:28; two examples of *forth-telling* are Ezekiel 37:1-14, Luke 5:22-24.)

Something else we need to keep in mind is that in ministry these gifts very often seem to intersect and flow together. And, when you are in the midst of ministry, it is not all that profitable to try to discern which gift God is using at any particular moment.

In some of the discussion, I will share some of my own personal experiences, and how I have seen God minister *to me* "prophetically" for my "*strengthening, encouragement and comfort*" (cf. 1 Corinthians 14:3); or how God ministered *through me* to someone else. It could be debated in each instance on "the purity" of the example in how it relates to the spiritual gift we discuss. The purpose of this lesson is not to debate, but to present to you how God may use each of these gifts to reveal His Heart to someone. I will let you decide for yourself what you consider to be prophetic or not. Let's begin ...

I. *The Gift of Prophecy*:

When I lived in the Pittsburgh, PA. area, I started taking a course on the prophetic at a church in the Columbus, OH area connected to Dr. Bill Hamon's ministries. They strongly encouraged us to practice what we were being taught. So, in a pastor's prayer group that met at the church where I pastored, I decided to "practice" on them! As I asked the Lord to give me a word to "*strengthen, encourage or comfort*" my friends, I believe I received something that was several sentences in length for all of them ... *except one*. All that I sensed that the Lord wanted me to say for one of my friends was, "*I have a place for you.*" And that was it! I did not try to "elaborate or interpret" that word, but simply spoke it to him as the Lord had given it to me.

Afterwards, I asked this pastor friend, if this word meant anything to him. He shared that for the past 2 weeks he had been asking the Lord if "*He had a place for him or not*", because of difficulties he was experiencing in his congregation at that time.

1) Can you think of a time when God *"strengthened, encouraged or comforted"* you with "timely words" that were spoken through someone else?

_____
_____
_____
_____
_____
_____

2) What are some things that may be keeping you from believing that God could prophesy through you to *"strengthen, encourage or comfort"* someone else?

_____
_____
_____
_____
_____
_____

II. *A Word of Knowledge:*

The Greek word used for *knowledge* (*gnosis*), implies, "the possession of information", and can also translate as, *"what is known, insight, understanding."* Through this spiritual gift, the Holy Spirit gives *"insight and information"* about someone (e.g., Matt.9:4; 22:18)

I became more personally aware of the revelatory nature of this gift at a gathering of Presbyterians involved with renewal. We also "practiced" ministering to each other. When it was my turn to be prayed for, *I was nervous*! At a key point in their ministry to me, one of the men present was given a "word-picture" and asked if it meant anything to me. He described very accurately and in detail my parents living room fireplace with the clock my dad had made hanging above the fireplace mantle and the two civil war rifles on either side of the clock.

I immediately thought of my dad. My dad had died about a year earlier, and I had never truly grieved for him. This *"word of knowledge"* allowed me to grieve his death, and, as a side result, I even received some physically healing for some of my allergies.

1) Can you think of a time when someone spoke a *word of knowledge* to you? Or through you to someone?

_____

_____

_____

_____

_____

_____

2) What are some things that may be keeping you from believing that God could speak a *word of knowledge* through you to *"strengthen, encourage or comfort"* someone else?

_____

_____

_____

_____

_____

_____

III. *A Word of Wisdom:*

The Greek word for *"wisdom"* (*sophia*) goes beyond *knowledge* and *insight* and becomes more the *use of the information* and "application". I realize that "wisdom" is subjective to the beholder. And even though I can think of many ministry situations where the Lord has helped me to know what to do connected to a word of knowledge given, I am going to use an example of Jesus taking a "word of knowledge" about someone, then speaking a "word of wisdom" into the situation.

Take a look at Matthew 22:15-22:

1) What *"insight"* does the Holy Spirit give about those who came to Him (cf. vs.15-18)? What *"application from God"* does the Holy Spirit give Jesus to speak into the situation?

_____
_____
_____
_____
_____
_____

2) How might it have *"strengthened, encouraged or comforted"* the different groups of people present?

_____
_____
_____
_____
_____
_____

3) When have you seen the Holy Spirit minister to you or someone else in this kind of "timely manner"?

_____

_____

_____

_____

_____

_____

_____

IV. *Discernment of Spirits*:

The Greek words for *"discernment of spirits"* could also be translated as "differentiate spirits"; that is, "which spirit is at work" - God's Spirit, human spirit or demonic spirit. I have been in ministry situations where it is very important to know what we are dealing with for the sake of the person receiving ministry. When Jesus healed people, not everything had a spiritual cause. But when there was a spiritual root - like sin in a person's life or a demonic oppressor - Jesus dealt with each situation uniquely and personal to the person. So should we.

As a word of warning, when you discern something like this, others may think you are "weird". Also our discernment might be considered very subjective and viewed with skepticism. So let's look at where the Apostle Paul both was given a *"discernment of spirits"* and, I also believe, *"a word of wisdom."*

Take a look at Acts 16:16-18:

1) What did the Holy Spirit show Paul about the "spiritual inspiration" in this "slave-girls" revelation? (The Greek words for *"spirit of divination/by which she predicted the future"* literally translates as "a python-spirit")

_____

_____

_____

_____

_____

2) Why was it important for Paul to know her source of "spiritual inspiration and revelation"?

_____

_____

_____

_____

_____

3) When have you seen the Holy Spirit minister to you or someone else in this kind of "strategic manner"?

_____

_____

_____

_____

_____

V. *The Interpretation of Tongues:*

I will briefly share three different personal experiences.

The Greek words for *interpretation of tongues* can also be translated as *translation of languages or utterances*. Paul also says, in 1 Corinthians 13:1 that there are "*tongues of men and of angels*". That is, some of the "utterances" we will hear will have a correspondence to "earthly languages", and some will have a heavenly correspondence. My experiences are more "earthly" than "heavenly".

#1: A group of us were praying for Presbyterian ministers from Taiwan. A phrase came to me in Chinese that I understood, since I have studied Chinese. I knew the English translation, but sensed I was supposed to say it to the pastors in Chinese, even though I felt embarrassed by my pronunciation. The way it was phrased in Chinese greatly excited the pastors and offered them encouragement for specific ministry opportunities they were praying about. My speaking the English translation would not have had the same impact. I spoke the word in a language I knew, and God had the interpretation with those to whom I spoke it.

#2: In another prayer ministry situation, we were praying for a woman who was from Japan. I have not studied Japanese, nor have I been to Japan. While we were praying for her, this foreign sounding word popped into my mind. I felt a little foolish, but spoke it as I "heard" it, and asked her if it meant anything... *It did!* It allowed us to minister to her in a very specific and strategic manner. I spoke a word in a language I did not know, and God had the interpretation and meaning with her.

#3: I have been in different meeting settings where someone spoke out in an "utterance or tongue" that was not "naturally known" to those present. In one particular

instance, it occurred at the church I pastored during a conference on Prayer Evangelism. I was up front in the leadership, and I had a strong sense of what had been said, even though I had absolutely know idea what language it was, earthly or otherwise. I spoke what I sensed God put on my heart, and heard after the meeting from many of those present that it "ministered" to them. In this case, it was a language I did not know or speak, yet God gave me the interpretation.

1) What has been your exposure to the spiritual gift *"interpretation of tongues"*?

_____

_____

_____

_____

_____

_____

2) What are some things that may be keeping you from believing that God could *speak a tongue* through you that someone else interprets, or *interpret a tongue* through you to *"strengthen, encourage or comfort"* someone else?

_____

_____

_____

_____

_____

_____

Close in Prayer for each other. If you desire to receive a particular spiritual gift that we have listed, *pray for them in faith* that the Holy Spirit wants to impart to them. But practice listening to the Holy Spirit as you pray.

LESSON 5 : Ways God Reveals His Heart to Us – Part 3 : "God Uses " The Testimony of Jesus"

The last sentence of Revelation 19:10 says, "For the testimony of Jesus is the spirit of prophecy." The scriptures are one source of the "testimony of Jesus"; His interaction with our lives is another source. When we "testify" to what Jesus has done or is doing it becomes a form of "prophetic revelation" that can *strengthen, encourage or comfort*. I have seen it happen. In some instances, the testimony of the healing of one person also "spoke into" the life of someone else *for their own healing*.

Three thoughts about what we are *NOT* saying:

1) We are *not* saying that we can use the scriptures or the testimonies of others to justify our actions.

2) We are *not* saying that we can use the scriptures or the testimonies of others like "magical incantations" or "divine formulas" to accomplish our desires.

3) We are *not* saying that this is anything that can be done by our own desire or strength.

Three thoughts about what we *ARE* saying:

1) We sense the Holy Spirit leading us to specific passages of scripture whose truths or applications "speak into" our specific situation for *"strengthening, encouragement or comfort."*

2) We sense the Holy Spirit leading us to the testimonies of others to "speak into" our situations for *"strengthening, encouragement or comfort."*

3) We then are lead either to "proclaim" or "pray" those truths into our situation as the Holy Spirit leads.

Two Examples from my own personal life.

I.   ***Read* Hosea 1:1-11**

Over the years, the Lord keeps leading me into contact with other spiritual leaders who have burden to see transformation take place through prophetic prayer and intercession. Some of this Prophetic Intercession has occurred for my denomination; some has occurred within the communities I have lived.

When I lived in Shippensburg, I have found myself involved with others who have a burden for our community. One of the unique characteristics of our town is that it is split between two counties - Cumberland County in the north, and Franklin County in the south. During one particular season of prayer for our community, one of these leaders was lead to Hosea 1:1-11 as "speaking into" our spiritual circumstances.

There are different aspects of this passage that we believe connects to the history of our area; especially vs.4 because of the "bloodshed" in this valley against the Native Americans committed by the early settlers. Furthermore, historically speaking, the churches in "the north" don't seem to interact with those in "the south" - our "kingdom" is divided, much like Israel was.

We believe the Holy Spirit led us to verses 10-11 in answer to our labor in prayer for God to restore us as His unified church within our community divided by two counties. We believe that the Lord spoke into our situation, and gave us a "testimony" of His word to proclaim and claim for our *"strengthening, encouragement or comfort."*

II.   *Read* Isaiah 16:5

The past decade plus, I have sensed the Lord leading me to deepen my intimacy with Him, and to deepen my understanding of His love for me. I have read about various people whom God used to bring about revival in the past, or whom God used to lead us into a new work of God in the present. King David and the Apostle John are two of my bible heroes and inspirations to pursue the love of God; Smith Wigglesworth is a revivalist I admire. One of the more recent testimonies I have read about intimacy with God is in Heidi Baker's book, *"Compelled by Love"*. A constant and common element that they all seem to testify about is having had a tangible experience of the presence and power of God's love. As I read about these men and women of faith and their close intimacy with God, my prayers have been, *"Do this with me Lord! I want to know your love more."*

Isaiah 16:5 is a verse of scripture and a testimony about Jesus I believe the Lord lead me to read so that it would speak into my life. It is a Messianic prophecy:

> *"In love a throne will be established; in faithfulness a man will sit on it - one from the house of David - one who in judging seeks justice and speeds the cause of righteousness."*

This verse speaks about the work Jesus Christ has begun and continues to work to complete *through us* and *within us* (cf. John 4:34). It is a verse that I have both "proclaimed" or "sown in prayer" as testimony to what Jesus is doing or wants to do with me, or wants to do in the lives of others, including my community.

It has been a "testimony of Jesus" that has spoken into my life for my *"strengthening, encouragement and comfort."*

Practical Application and Prayer for Vision

1) Take some time now and go before the Lord on behalf of your community. Ask the Lord to show you what your community is like. Then ask the Lord what is on His Heart for your community.

2) Ask the Lord to lead you to a passage of scripture that speaks His Heart for your community. Then ask the Lord what He would have you do with this passage - proclaim it, or sow it into your community through prayer.

LESSON 6 : Ways God Reveals His Heart to Us – Part 4 : "God Uses Dreams and Visions"

In Acts 2:16-18, the Apostle Peter quotes from Joel 2:28 on the day of Pentecost to interpret what people are seeing take place before their eyes.

> 16 *No, this is what was spoken by the prophet Joel:* 17 *"In the last days, God says, I will pour out my Spirit on all people. Your sons and daughters will prophesy, your young men will see visions, your old men will dream dreams.* 18 *Even on my servants, both men and women, I will pour out my Spirit in those days, and they will prophesy."* (Acts 2:16-18)

Dreams and visions are connected to the prophetic. Both the Old and New Testaments give us many examples of this truth. For the sake of simplicity in introducing this subject to you, I am going to present the categories and definitions used by Kris Vallotton in his book, ***Basic Training for the Prophetic Ministry.*** Kris describes two types of visions - *visions of the mind* and *open visions*; and two types of dreams - *virtual reality dreams* and *reality dreams.*

We will talk about these four types of prophetic communications below. But before we do, we must keep in mind some important points Kris challenges his readers with about *dreams* that also applies to *visions* (Chapter 4, pg. 43). To summarize:

1) *"Not all dreams are from God"*. It is

important that we discern the source of our *dreams* and *visions*.

2) Powerful dreams don't make us prophetic. God also gave *dreams* to those who did not know Him as "warnings". What makes us prophetic is the *interpretation* of the dreams.

3) Symbolic images are important to the interpretation of the *dreams* as they also can be with *visions*. But ultimately it is God who interprets, and we need to let Him speak His interpretation to us in both.

4) Many opportunities to benefit from *dreams* and *visions* God gives may be missed because we are not prepared to make a record it. Keep something handy to *write with* and *write upon*.

5) If you are interested in growing in this area of the prophetic, then ask the Lord to speak to you in these ways. Kris offers a simple prayer we can pray: *"Your servant is listening."*

I. God's Use of *Virtual Reality Dreams*:

Kris defines a *virtual reality dream* as a dream that "remains in our mind after waking" and is often "symbolic and needs interpretation" (Chapter 4, pg. 41). Let's look at two examples:

A. Genesis 37:5-11: Joseph's Dreams Two Dreams of Greatness.

1. Describe each of the two dreams. Who has the interpretation of each dream?

2. How did Joseph's family members respond to each dream? Why?

3. What do you believe to be God's purpose for giving Joseph these two dreams?

B. Genesis 41:9-16, 28-40: Joseph's Interpretation of Pharaoh's Dreams.

1. Describe each of the two dreams. Who has the interpretation of each dream?

2. How did Pharaoh respond to Joseph's interpretation of the two dreams? Why?

3. What do you see to be the difference between the Joseph of Genesis 37:5-11, and the Joseph of Genesis 41?

4. What have you learnt about God's desire for us in giving dreams and their interpretation?

II. God's Use of *Reality Dreams*:

Kris defines a *reality dream* as "a real experience we have while sleeping that we remember after waking" (Chapter 4, pg. 41). Kris refers to two examples of a *reality dream*:

A) Genesis 20:1-7,12: God Comes to Abimelech in a Dream.

1. Describe the situation. Why do you think God chose to "prophesy" to King Abimelech in this manner?

2. What do you believe are God's "prophetic purposes" for this dream?

3. What does this tell you about the Heart of God? God's Heart for you?

B) Matthew 2:13-19: An Angel of the Lord Appears to Joseph.

      1. Describe the situation. Why do you think God chose to "prophesy" to Joseph in this manner?

      2. What do you believe are God's "prophetic purposes" for this dream?

      3. What does this tell you about the Heart of God?

III. God's Use of *Visions of the Mind*:

      Kris defines *visions of the mind* as when "the Lord *'projects'* images and pictures onto the *'screen'* of our minds"(Chapter 4, pg. 39). Let's look at one particular example:

Note: There could be overlap between *visions of the mind*, *virtual reality dreams,* and the spiritual gift *word of knowledge*. I chose this example because, like some others, it happens *in the night* and is not called a "dream."

A. Acts 16:6-10: Paul's Vision of the Man of Macedonia.

Note: The first convert Paul made in Europe was Lydia a "seller of purple" who resided in Philippi, the chief city in the eastern division of Macedonia (cf. Acts 16:13-15).

1. What are some of the ways you see the Holy Spirit guiding the Apostle Paul and his companions? What might be frustrating about trusting the Holy Spirit in this way?

_____

_____

_____

_____

_____

_____

2. What do you see as God's purposes in leading Paul in this manner?

_____

_____

_____

_____

_____

_____

IV. God's Use of *Open Visions*:

Kris defines an *open vision* as when we "see with [our] natural eyes" (Chapter 4, pg. 39).

A. Acts 10:9-23: Peter's Vision's

1. Describe Peter's vision and the images and symbolism in it.

_____

_____

_____

2. Compare this passage with Acts 12:9. What do you learn about "visions" from this comparison?

_____

_____

_____

3. How many times did the Holy Spirit interpret this vision in Acts 10:9-23 for Peter? What are the different ways the Holy Spirit brought Peter the interpretation?

_____

_____

_____

4. Why do you think the Lord gave the interpretation of this vision in stages?

_____

_____

_____

Summary:

1. What have you learned about *dreams* from the Lord in this study?

_____

_____

_____

2. What have you learned about *visions* from the Lord in this study?

_____

_____

_____

3. **Close in prayer** for each other - ask the Lord to open up your heart, mind and spirit to His *dreams* and *visions* for you, and for His Spirit to *gift* you with interpretation as well.

SECTION 3 : "Living a Prophetic Lifestyle"

LESSON 7: Living a Prophetic Lifestyle:

"Ministering to Others Prophetically"

LESSON 7 : Living a Prophetic Lifestyle: "Ministering to Others Prophetically"

In this lesson, we will be looking at two things: 1) Some *"words of wisdom"* as you begin to explore *Living a Prophetic Lifestyle*; and, 2) Some ways that you can begin to let the Holy Spirit guide you with some suggested "Listening Prayer" Exercises.

Some *"Words of Wisdom"*:

1) <u>Let your ministry flow from your intimacy with the Lord</u>:

> "19 *We love because he first loved us.* 20 *If anyone says, "I love God," yet hates his brother, he is a liar. For anyone who does not love his brother, whom he has seen, cannot love God, whom he has not seen."*
>
> (1 John 4:19-20)

The *flow* of our ministry will spring from the *fruit* of our relationship with the Lord.

How is the quality and quantity of your time *alone* with the Lord?

_____

_____

_____

2) <u>Be under authority and accountable to spiritual leadership over you</u>:

> "*Obey your leaders and submit to their authority. They keep watch over you as men who must give an account.*

Obey them so that their work will be a joy, not a burden, for that would be of no advantage to you." (Hebrews 13:17)

1 Corinthians 14 and 1 John 4:1 both stress the importance of "testing" what comes out from both prophets and prophecy. You cannot test or be tested if there is no accountability.

Are you accountable to someone else in the Lord? To a local congregation, and/or prophetic ministry?

_____
_____
_____

3) <u>It is better - and more enjoyable - not to minister alone:</u>

*"Calling the Twelve to him, he **sent them out** two by two ..."* (Mark 6:7)

*"**Two are better** than one, because they have a good return for their work:"* (Ecclesiastes 4:9)

This is not always possible. But, whenever possible, either take someone with you, or go with someone who is also learning about the prophetic.

Can you think of someone with whom you can minister and seek the Holy Spirit's guidance?

_____
_____
_____

4) <u>Avoid words of condemnation and accusation:</u>

"But everyone who prophesies speaks to men for their

strengthening, encouragement and comfort."
(1 Corinthians 14:3)

Remember what the Apostle Paul instructs us to be the purpose of prophecy. If you sense something that is outside these guidelines, ask the Lord if you are being influenced by your temperament or your situation. Also ask the Lord how you might be able to speak His Life and Heart into the person. This is another reason why it may be good to go with a partner.

Do you have struggles with anger and bitterness? How would others describe your personality and temperament? Are you willing to ask someone you respect?

_____

_____

_____

5) You *sow what you grow*:

"Let us not become weary in doing good, for at the proper time we will reap a harvest if we do not give up."
(Galatians 6:9)

Our gifts are strengthened as we exercise them. But the enemy will work to keep you from exercising your gifts. So don't walk out your call based upon how you are received. Rather, stay close to the Lord's Heart, and you will be able press through difficult circumstances. Ask the Lord to begin giving you opportunities to minister His *"strengthening, encouragement and comfort"* to others? Then be willing to step out in faith!

On the next few pages are some "Listening Prayer" exercises that can help you can exercise and practice *Living a Prophetic Lifestyle.*

Listening Prayer Exercises

Purpose:

1) <u>Level #1:</u> To provide "practice opportunities" in *Listening and Discernment* for how the Lord speaks to us in a "safe environment" - one-on-one, small group, or classroom training exercises.

2) <u>Level #2::</u> To provide "practice opportunities" in *Listening and Discernment* for how the Lord speaks to us in "every-day-life" situations - opportunities for evangelism and being a witness for Jesus Christ; opportunities for ministry.

<u>*Note:*</u> These are either *"listening and discerning"* exercises that I have been taught by others, I have come up with myself, or adapted from what others have done.

Level #1 Listening and Discernment Exercises

<u>*Exercise* #1:</u> ("one-on-one" exercises)

1. Find a partner with whom to pray.

2. Both of you ask the Holy Spirit to guide you and speak to you. Ask the Holy Spirit to anoint each of you so that you will be able to speak something that might *"strengthen, encourage, or comfort"* your prayer partner (cf. 1 Corinthians 14:3).

3. Wait and listen to the Lord *believing that the Lord wants to show you something* for your prayer partner.

4. *After 3 minutes* - take the risk to share any "impressions, words, sensations, or word pictures" you believe the Lord may

have given you for them.

> - Start off by saying, *"I believe the Lord showed me this for you* .... (then share what you believe the Lord showed you).

> - Then, after you have shared, ask your prayer partner if that seems to connect with what is going on in their life, or with what the Lord is/has-been doing in their life.

> - If you don't have any "sense of impression" for them, *that's alright!* Let your partner share, if they do, then you can repeat the exercise.

5. If the Lord shows you something that might *"strengthen, encourage, or comfort"* your prayer partner, then *turn it into a prayer for them.*

Exercise #2: ("one-on-one" exercises)

1. *Except for the class leader,* form two lines and have each person close their eyes and turn their backs to the people in the other line.

2. The class leader will then move the people around in one of the lines with the object of not letting each line know who is now standing behind them.

3. Each person in the line chosen will ask the Holy Spirit to guide them, and to anoint them so that they will be able to spea something that might *"strengthen, encourage, or comfort"* the person behind them that they cannot see (cf. 1 Corinthians 14:. You can also ask each line to do this for the person behind them.

4. *After 3 minutes* - have the two lines of people open their ey

and face each other, and have them share any "impressions, words, sensations, or word pictures" you believe the Lord may have given you for them. Start off by saying, *"I believe the Lord showed me this for you* .... (then share what you believe the Lord showed you).

Exercise #3: ("one-on-one" exercises)

1. Find a partner with whom to pray. Each of you should have a note-pad and something to write with.

2. Both of you ask the Holy Spirit to guide you and speak to you. Ask the Holy Spirit to anoint each of you so that you will be able to speak something that might *"strengthen, encourage, or comfort"* your prayer partner (cf. 1 Corinthians 14:3).

3. Wait and listen to the Lord *believing that the Lord wants to show you something* for your prayer partner. Write down or describe what you believe the Lord is "impressing" upon your heart and mind for them.

4. *After 3 minutes* - take the risk to share any "impressions, words, sensations, or word pictures" you believe the Lord may have given you for them.

> - Start off by saying, *"I believe the Lord showed me this for you* .... (then share what you believe the Lord showed you).

> - Then, after you have shared, ask your prayer partner if that seems to connect with what is going on in their life, or with what the Lord is/has-been doing in their life.

> - If you don't have any "sense of impression" for them, *that's alright!* Let your partner share, if they do, then you can repeat the exercise.

5. If the Lord shows you something that might *"strengthen, encourage, or comfort"* your prayer partner, then *turn it into a prayer for them.*

Exercise #4: ("Triad" exercise)

- Repeat exercise #1, but done in "groups of three". Take a little bit more time to *listen and discern*, but not much more than five minutes.

Exercise #5: ("Triad" exercise)

- Repeat exercise #3, but done in "groups of three". Take a little bit more time to *listen and discern*, but not much more than five minutes.

Exercise #6: ("Class room" exercise)

1. The Class Leader will choose someone from the classroom, but *not* tell the class room who this person is.

2. The Class Leader will ask the Holy Spirit to guide them, and to anoint them so that they will be able to speak something that might *"strengthen, encourage, or comfort"* the person the Class Leader has chosen (cf. 1 Corinthians 14:3).

3. *After 3 minutes* - the Class Leader will ask each person in the class to share any *impressions* or *words* they believe the Lord gave to them.

> - The Class Leader will write it down on a chalk board, white board, butcher paper for everyone to see, noting patterns or similar impressions in what is being spoken

> - Each person will start off by saying, *"I believe the Lo*

showed me this for them .... (then share what you believe the Lord showed you).

4. *After everyone has had the opportunity to share*, the Class Leader will reveal who the "mystery student" is, and ask if that seems to connect with what is going on in their life, or with what the Lord is/has-been doing in their life.

5. Have the Class Leader turn it into a prayer for them.

6. Repeat the exercise with someone else being chosen by the Class Leader.

Exercise #7: ("Class" Exercise in a church setting - *more advanced*)

1. The Class Leader will ask the Holy Spirit to guide them, and to anoint them with the necessary *insight and discernment they will need.*

2. Send the students out into the church building with notepads and something to write with. The students will walk around the building they are in *for approximately 30 minutes* making notes of their *discernment for the various rooms*, then return to the class room. *They are NOT to talk to anyone else* during this time period.

3. Have "butcher/construction paper" in several places upon the walls.

4. Have students share "one at a time", and, if possible, have a separate sheet for the different rooms they received an *impression or discernment* for.

- Each person will start off by saying, *"I believe the Lord showed me this for them* .... (then share what you believe the Lord showed you).

- Compile what the students believe they have *discerned*.

- Turn it into prayer for the church respecting the "spiritual authority" of the church's leadership.

Exercise #8: ("Class" Exercise in a church setting - *more advanced*)

1. Ahead of time, photo copy/print up "flags of nations" from around the world - select a minimum of 12 and no more than twenty - "colored copies" preferred; *don't forget to put the names of the nations on the flag.* (Some churches actually have flags hanging in their sanctuaries.)

2. The Class Leader will ask the Holy Spirit to guide them, and to anoint them with the necessary *insight and discernment they will need.*

3. Send the students out into the church building with notepads and something to write with. The students will walk around the room with the flags, stopping at each one *for no more than 1 minute* making notes of any *impressions or discernment* they believe the Lord has given them for that particular flag,

4. Have "butcher/construction paper" in several places upon the walls of the room where you are meeting.

5. Have students share "one at a time", and, if possible, have a separate sheet for the different rooms they received an *impression or discernment* for.

- Each person will start off by saying, *"I believe the Lo*
showed me this for them .... (then share what you belie

the Lord showed you).

- Compile what the students believe they have discerned.

- Turn it into prayer for those nations - let each person choose the nation they believe they should pray for, and gather into groups for that particular nation.

Exercise #9: (Personal Discernment and Prayer Exercise - *more advanced*)

1. Ahead of time, the Class Leader will get cell phone numbers of people in the church or not in the church, ones that are hopefully "unknown" to their students but hopefully "remembered" by the Class Leader.

2. At the end of a class session, give each student a pre-selected cell phone number.

- They have one week to complete the assignment (or until the next class);

- Ask the Holy Spirit to anoint you so that you will be able to speak something that might *"strengthen, encourage, or comfort"* the person to whom you will be calling (cf. 1 Corinthians 14:3).

- Wait and listen to the Lord *believing that the Lord wants to show you something* for the person to whom you will be calling.

- Then call them (don't forget to identify yourself and share what you are doing!) Share what you believe the Lord has shown you for them; then ask if it "connects" for what the Lord is doing in their lives.

- Close in prayer with them.

3. Report back to the class what the Lord showed you.

   - *By faith*, walk up to the person to whom you are led, introduce yourself and mention what you believe the Lord put on your heart for them.

   - It is possible that the Lord puts nothing specific on your heart for them *except to ask if you can pray for them.* If that happens, then ask them if they have anything you could pray for them.

   - You can do this by yourself, with a partner, or up to about three people.

Level #2 Listening and Discernment Exercises

Exercise #1: (Personal Discernment and Prayer Exercise - *more advanced*)

    - Go to a store, and ask the Lord to lead you to someone whom He would have you pray for.

    - Ask the Holy Spirit to anoint you so that you will be able to speak something that might *"strengthen, encourage, or comfort"* the person to whom the Lord leads you (cf. 1 Corinthians 14:3).

    - *By faith*, walk up to the person to whom you are led, introduce yourself and mention what you believe the Lord put on your heart for them.

    - It is possible that the Lord puts nothing specific on your heart for them *except to ask if you can pray for them.* If that happens, then ask them if they have anything you could pray for them.

    - *Don't look like you are stalking people!*

    - You can do this by yourself, or with a partner.

    - *Be safe* in how you do this!

Exercise #2: (Personal Discernment and Prayer Exercise - *more advanced*)

    - Go to a restaurant with someone for a meal.

    - Ask the Holy Spirit to anoint you so that you will be able to speak something that might *"strengthen, encourage, or comfort"* the person to whom Lord leads you (cf. 1 Corinthians 14:3).

- *If is the waiter/waitress, don't forget to tip them generously!*

Exercise #3: (Personal Discernment and Prayer Exercise – *more advanced*)

- Ask the Lord to give you a telephone number of someone whom He wants you to minister. Follow the same steps in prayer, faith and discernment as in previous exercises.

Exercise #4: (Personal Discernment and Prayer Exercise - *more advanced*)

- In a group of two or three, ask the Lord to show you a business person or public official in your community that He would have you pray for.

- Pray together before you go, then make an appointment to see them.

- When you meet with them, identify yourselves, then share what you believe the Lord has put upon your heart that might *"strengthen, encourage, or comfort"* the person to whom Lord leads you to (cf. 1 Corinthians 14:3).

- *Then ask if you can pray for them.*

Closing Notes:

1. There are "endless possibilities" for how the Lord could use each of us *if we would only listen to Him*, believing that He *can* use us, and *wants* to use us!

2. As Jesus said, in Matthew 9:35-38,

> 35 *Jesus went through all the towns and villages, teaching in their synagogues, preaching the good news of the kingdom and healing every disease and sickness. 36 When he saw the crowds, he had compassion on them, because they were harassed and helpless, like sheep without a shepherd. 37 Then he said to his disciples, "The harvest is plentiful but the workers are few. 38 Ask the Lord of the harvest, therefore, to send out workers into his harvest field."*

3. Make *Listening Prayer* a **"life-style-choice",** not just a "program" or a "religious activity" that you pull off a shelf every once in a while. Then don't be surprised if your community starts changing... if *you* start to change and grow in the Lord!

Prayer Journal

Date: Need: Date Answered:

DENNY FINNEGAN'S OTHER WORKBOOKS

FOUNDATIONS : Understanding Prayer Ministry
Prayer Ministry in the Local Church
ISBN: 978-0-615-34744-8 52895
Excellent Adventures! Inc. Press

Foundation Series:
Intercessory Prayer Mini-Course
Growing Personally As An Intercessor
ISBN: 978-0-9889584-0-1 Kindle version
ISBN: 978-0-9889584-3-2 Paperback version

Foundation Series:
Healing Prayer Mini-Course
Living the Healing Ministry of Jesus
ISBN: 978-0-9889584-2-5 Kindle version
ISBN: 978-0-9889584-4-9 Paperback version

Foundation Series:
Prophetic Prayer Mini-Course
Living a Prophetic Lifestyle
ISBN: 978-0-9889584-1-8 Kindle version
ISBN: 978-0-9889584-5-6 Paperback version

70042461R00042

Made in the USA
Columbia, SC
28 April 2017